SHE'S BEEN WORKING ON THE
RAILROAD

Also by Nancy Smiler Levinson

Turn of the Century
Our Nation One Hundred Years Ago

Christopher Columbus
Voyager to the Unknown

I Lift My Lamp
Emma Lazarus and the Statue of Liberty

SHE'S BEEN WORKING ON THE
RAILROAD

by NANCY SMILER LEVINSON

photos collected and taken by
SHIRLEY BURMAN

LODESTAR BOOKS
Dutton   New York

Library of Congress Cataloging-in-Publication Data

Levinson, Nancy Smiler.
    She's been working on the railroad / text by Nancy Smiler Levinson; photos collected and taken by Shirley Burman.—1st ed.
        p.   cm.
    Includes bibliographical references (pp. 98–99) and index.
    Summary: Relates the story of women who have worked on the railroad in ever-increasing numbers and expanding range of jobs from the mid-1800s to the present.
    ISBN 0-525-67545-0 (alk. paper)
    1. Women railroad employees—United States—History—Juvenile literature.
[1. Women railroad employees.   2. Railroads.]
I. Title.
HD6073.R12U65   1997
331.4'81385'0973—dc21   97-1058   CIP   AC

Published in the United States by Lodestar Books,
an affiliate of Dutton Children's Books,
a member of Penguin Putnam Inc.,
375 Hudson Street, New York, New York 10014

Published simultaneously in Canada
by McClelland & Stewart, Toronto

Editor: Virginia Buckley   Designer: Dick Granald

Printed in the U.S.A.   First Edition
10   9   8   7   6   5   4   3   2   1

In celebration of my twenty years of association with them, I dedicate this book to the Society of Children's Book Writers and Illustrators.

N.S.L.

This book is dedicated to Richard Steinheimer, my husband, who generously supported and assisted me in my research, writing, and photography during many years of assembling materials on women's contributions to the railroad industry.

S.B.

Acknowledgments

Gratitude is expressed to the many people who assisted during the preparation, photograph collecting, and writing of this book.

Bonnie and Perry Adams were generous in sharing their work and knowledge from the earliest days of research. Jeanne McDonald, founder of Women's Heritage Museum, was especially supportive.

Sharing their stories were Ida Stevens Petersen, Ruth Morgan Weitkamp, Mary Ellen Cookman Day, Jocelyn Wagner Knowles, Christene Gonzales Aldeis, Linda Niemann, Julie Watson, Barbara Perry, Leah Rosenfeld, Lillian Tamoria, Anne Hazell, Magda Ratajski, and Maggie Silver.

Helping with expertise and research were Connie Menninger, Santa Fe Railway collections archivist, Kansas State Historical Society; Karen Bartlett, Nemesis Productions; Robert Hoppe, *Southern Pacific Bulletin*; John Gruber, editor, *Vintage Rails* magazine; George Drury, librarian and archivist, *Trains* magazine; Thomas C. Jepsen, telegraph historian; Rebecca Burcher, editor, *Norfolk Southern Focus* magazine; Michele Stelter, ACRW member and Trailer Train Corporation; Anne Bennof, American Association of Railroads; John Hankey, historian and former curator, B&O Railroad Museum; Anne Calhoun, photo archivist, B&O Railroad Museum; W. Oliver Gibson; Stan Kistler; Guy Dunscomb; John Signor; Jeffrey Moreau, author and railroad photo collector; John H. White and William L. Withuhn, Smithsonian Institution; Janice Griffith, La Posada Foundation; Catherine Taylor, California State Railroad Museum foundation director, as well as museum staff members Richard Denison, Marilyn Sommerdorf, Kevin Bunker, Stephen Drew, and Ellen Halteman.

Thanks are also due to Nancy Ferrell, Mina A. Jacobs, Barbara Wicker, Hyde Branch Library; Joyce Adgate, Centre County Historical Library and Museum; Kitty Deernose, Little Bighorn Custer Battlefield National Monument; Bruce Heard, National Railroad Passenger Corporation (Amtrak).

Contents

THE IRON HORSE

When steam engine locomotives first began to chug and puff along short distances of track in America in the 1830s, people called them iron horses. Some worried about dangers they might cause and warned mothers to keep their children away from railway crossings. Others saw them only as novelty inventions for little more than amusement.

But railroads grew at a rapid pace and quickly replaced the horse and stagecoach. Soon they crisscrossed the land, hauling logs, raw materials, and farm produce. By the end of the nineteenth century, trains, trailing great puffs of smoke and blowing their loud whistles, streaked across two hundred thousand miles of steel track. Railroads had become one of the biggest and most profitable businesses in America, and they helped to turn it into a powerful industrial nation.

The railroads were owned, built, and run by men. The owners were ambitious and competitive, and not always wholly honest in their business dealings. They hired laborers who toiled at the enormous tasks of leveling the ground and laying the tracks. The engineers, conductors, brakemen, firemen, station agents, dispatchers, and numerous other workers needed to keep the railroads operating were all men.

But women also have a history on the American railroad. There were only a few in limited positions at first, but in time their numbers rose, and they began to hold a range of jobs, which continued to expand throughout the years. Today, a great many women are employed alongside men in positions from skilled labor to management.

Their story begins in 1838, when a handful of white, Native American, and black (free or slaves-for-hire) women were employed in domestic service jobs. They also served water to thirsty passengers or sold fruit to women traveling in ladies' cars.

The earliest known names come from a Baltimore & Ohio Railroad employment record, which noted that in 1855 Bridget Doheny, Catherine Shirley, and Susan Morningstar worked as charwomen, cleaning the Camden depot on the B & O line. An 1870 Hartford & New Haven line payroll recorded that a Mrs. T. Hatch looked after the Newington, Connecticut, depot for seventy-five cents a day. And in a book by an old-timer, Herbert Hamblen, there is mention of a kindhearted boss who, upon the death of a car repairer, hired the dead man's poor widow and two of his children as "car-cleaning crew members."

For the most part, however, names and stories of early-day female railroad workers are forever lost to history.

In the last decades of the nineteenth century, women began to be hired as railroad telegraphers. Some of them also worked as ticket sellers and train dispatchers. At the turn of the century, many started to fill clerical posts. Also, one woman became president of a small narrow-gauge railway that was built to haul gold ore. There was one woman who improved car refrigeration, and another who worked as an architect, designing depots and track-side hotels.

During the two world wars, when men were sent to fight overseas, women back home were recruited to take their places in the industrial workforce, especially in war production plants. For the first time, thousands of wives, sisters, and daughters won railroad jobs that men had never imagined they could fill. At the start, they were hired mostly as clerks, service providers (such as laundresses or kitchen aides), and machinists. Later, retaining the traditional job titles, they succeeded as dispatchers, towermen, crossing flagmen, yardmasters, drawbridge tenders, steam-hammer and turntable operators, welders, brakemen, and freight handlers. Eventually, nearly three decades after World War II, several mastered careers as engineers on major railroads, controlling locomotives that weighed over two hundred tons, carried forty or fifty loaded cars, and ran at sixty miles an hour.

Women railroaders have not always been accepted or welcomed by their bosses or the men with whom they work side by side. These women have long struggled against prejudice and stereotyping regarding their place in the labor force. But their story is a remarkable one of many successful gains, and they have made a unique contribution to the history of our nation.

BRASS POUNDERS

One evening back in the 1870s, Ella Campbell, a young woman in Pennsylvania, sat at work at the Sligo Junction railroad depot. She was a telegraph operator, who sent and received coded messages between stations to help control railway traffic and avoid collisions.

According to Ella's schedule, an eastbound passenger train was due into the station soon. But to her surprise a freight train of heavily loaded cars pulled into the station, *westbound.*

After a brief stop, the conductor gave his engineer a shout and a wave to go ahead. When Ella realized that the train was about to proceed, she suddenly remembered hearing a few subtle quick clicks on her telegraph earlier in the evening. She was sure that she had heard an order for the freight train to remain at Sligo Junction.

She rushed out to the platform and told the conductor, but he argued, "No, that can't be. We have the right-of-way."

Ella insisted that she had heard correctly and that he should have received the message at the last station he passed in Troy. Finally, she persuaded the conductor to go inside the depot while she tapped a pattern of clicking sounds on her brass telegraph key, sending a message to her superintendent to check the order.

Just as the superintendent replied that the order to hold the freight train was correct, Ella, the conductor, and the freight engineer outside in his locomotive heard a whistle. It was the passenger train. With lightning speed, the engineer switched from the main track onto a siding track. He made it just in time as the other train pulled in. Ella's telegraphic skills and keenly trained ear had helped to head off a tragic collision.

The telegraph was the invention of Samuel Morse. It was the first means of communication by electricity. The Morse code was a system of short and long electrical signals (dots and dashes) that represented alphabet letters and punctuation marks. The sending operator pressed a key up and down to send the signals. The receiving operator used a device called a sounder, which caused an electromagnet to attract an iron bar. When the bar struck the electromagnet, a sharp instrument clicked corresponding dots and dashes onto a strip of paper. The receiving operator then decoded or "read" the message. In Ella's day, many telegraphers no longer used paper strips. They "read" letters and words by listening to click sounds only, and they wrote out those messages in their own hand.

Ella Campbell was one of many women of her time who worked the Morse system on the railroad. Their count is not known because records were inaccurate and incomplete, but most women hired by railway companies in the nineteenth century were telegraph operators.

Operators were also called brass pounders and later simply "ops." Whether they were women or men (by far in the majority), they were among the most crucial of all railroad employees.

Many early telegraph operators made their station or depot offices more homey by adding flowers and pictures to the walls.
HARPER'S MONTHLY AUGUST 1873, THOMAS C. JEPSEN COLLECTION

Accidents and deaths from any number of causes—boiler blowups, blizzards, collapsing bridges, the dangerous work of coupling cars, runaway trains—were already horror enough. But without traffic-controlling operators, hundreds more accidents, mostly spectacular collisions, would have occurred every year.

One historian wrote, "The telegraphic method of train operation was the greatest single step taken by railroads in their formative era."[1]

To become a skilled operator required training and experience. The work of sending and receiving was always demanding. Sometimes it meant verifying confusing messages. More often, it consisted of writing out orders for conductors and engineers of trains approaching the operator's station—instructing the trainmen exactly where to stop and when. These orders came from dispatchers. Frequently, block operators would "hand them up" to a passing train by way of a long-handled hoop that engineers and conductors could grab by hooking an arm through the hoop as their trains sped by. For small-town operators, the job often meant also working as station agent, which included bookkeeping and selling tickets.

A locomotive streaks past the railroad station, as the young "op" hands up the train orders to the fireman. RAILROAD STORIES SEPTEMBER 1935, SHIRLEY BURMAN COLLECTION

The earliest women brass pounders usually learned the craft from their fathers. Sisters Fannie and Julia Wheeler received lessons from their father in Vinton, Iowa, in the late 1860s when he was station agent for the Burlington, Cedar Rapids & Minnesota Railroad. Although the younger sister, Julia, eventually gave up her telegraph career to enroll in school, Fannie continued to advance her position as she moved from city to city. An Iowa newspaper wrote that Fannie "is regarded as one of the best operators in the country." The article also noted that "on one occasion she received 140 messages, without a single break—a feat which, probably, not one operator in a hundred could perform!"[2]

Eula Brown's father worked for the Houston & Texas Central line at the Mt. Airy and Iredell, Texas, stations, and he started teaching her when she was only eight years old. By tapping out the alphabet codes one letter at a time, she also learned to spell.

Some women learned from station agents, husbands, and eventually, telegraphy schools. Ellen Laughton was taught by an office manager in Dover, New Hampshire, and since she was "unusually quick and intelligent," she took over his position when he went to work in a bank soon afterward. Ellen was then fourteen years old.

Cassie Hill, who had come to California in a covered wagon when she was a child, replaced her husband at his Southern Pacific Railroad job following his death in 1884. She worked as ticket agent and operator at the Roseville depot so that she could support herself and five children.

Occasionally, women taught others the skills they had learned. Abbie Vaughan Strubel, one of the first women operators in the country, taught Morse code to her husband and their four children. The family's home was in a Pittsburgh division station of the Baltimore & Ohio Railroad, and the story goes that whenever a call came in, whoever was nearest the telegraph responded.

Andrew Carnegie, the steel manufacturer, worked as an operator for the Pennsylvania Railroad when he was young, and he later rose to a position where he hired other telegraphers for his office. In his autobiography he wrote: "Among all the new occupations invaded by women I do not know of any better suited for them than that of telegraph operator."[3] One of the first females he hired was a cousin, Maria Hogan. She became so efficient that Carnegie sent other women to her to learn, and her Pittsburgh freight station office gradually turned into a school.

Keeping a railroad running smoothly at all times was, of course, impossible. One night in the Sierra Nevada mountains in California a snowstorm knocked out the wires at the Truckee depot on the Southern Pacific line. The operator, known only as Miss Woods, couldn't get any orders for trains coming through.

Miss Woods took charge in the emergency. She made a schedule chart of her own, threw a shawl around her shoulders, put on boots and mittens, and grabbed a lantern. She went out into the snowy night to send some trains through and hold others back, managing all the while to keep order without major mishap.

Brass pounders had few dull moments on the job. Often their shifts, or "tricks," were filled with excitement. People viewed them with wonder, almost believing that they possessed a secret knowledge.

Even though they were paid less than men, women were generally respected for working outside of the home because of the importance of the job. For railway companies, they were considered "bargains" because they were honest, productive, dependable, and accepted low pay. Most of them took their jobs out of necessity to help their families.

A few women telegraphers became station agents prior to 1900 because some stations were so small that only one person was needed. If a woman sold tickets or handled freight shipments in addition to operating a telegraph, she was considered a station agent.
JEFFREY MOREAU COLLECTION

In 1869, a man named Robert Harris worked for the Chicago, Burlington & Quincy line in the railway's station in Earl, Illinois. While many men opposed hiring women, he felt sympathetic toward them, understanding that they had "few avenues of support." In an experiment, he hired Minnie Rockwell as an operator for ten dollars a week.

But a few days later, his supervisor decided that Miss Rockwell was not competent and that she complained too much about the depot being dirty. He also said that she was such a curiosity that "rowdy people" came to gawk at her, which disrupted the office routine. The records didn't show whether she was fired or she quit, but Robert Harris's experiment came to a quick end.

There lived in Hyde Park, Massachusetts, a young girl of fourteen, Lizzie Clapp. In the family were her mother and father, who was a painter and wallpaper hanger, and five sisters and brothers. When Mr. Clapp met with hard business times, Lizzie learned the telegraph in order to help out, and she was hired at the Hyde Park Readville station of the Boston & Providence Railroad.

One summer afternoon four years later, in 1876, Lizzie was sitting at her desk in front of an open window. When a thunderstorm came up, she took care to "cut the telegraph instrument out of circuit" by affixing a "lightning arrester" device between the instrument and the electric current power line. That was a safety measure to prevent lightning from following the power line wires inside.

But a discharge of lightning flashed through the window on a draft of wind, striking Lizzie, who was seated in the path of the electrical charge. She was instantly killed.

After Lizzie's untimely death, telegraphers everywhere were advised to take special precautions during thunderstorms. The message, printed in a magazine, *The Telegrapher*, acknowledged the hazards of the job and affirmed the continuing importance of railroad telegraphy work.[4]

While Lizzie Clapp's story ended tragically, other tales of the telegraph are heroic, exciting, and sometimes amusing. The tales that have been handed down to us are all part of the unfolding history of the early women brass pounders.

Ida Hewitt
Locomotive Engineer

Ida Hewitt lived in the wooded, hilly region of Ritchie County, West Virginia. Her father was a locomotive engineer on the Calico Railroad, a short line, narrow-gauge set of rails built at a narrower width than the standard gauge used by most railroads.

The Calico stretched twenty miles from the Ritchie asphalt mines to the town of Cairo. Two connected locomotives, called a doubleheader, hauled eight cars of asphalt up a steep grade and out of the valley. At Cairo, the train connected with the Baltimore & Ohio Railroad, which shipped the asphalt to cities for paving roads.

The train maintenance shop was near the Hewitts' house, and Ida often played there as a child. In time, she learned about the mechanics of locomotives. She rode along with her father, who taught her how to refuel the locomotive and handle the throttle to control the engine's speed.

The company also employed another engineer. One day when he fell ill, Ida, who was twenty-four, offered to take his place until he recovered. But the man never recovered, and by the time he died, Ida had become so able an engineer that the Calico hired her.

Ida was known to wear a blue cotton suit, blue cap, and heavy shoes and gloves. "Her locomotive is neater than a man's," a local fellow remarked, "and she has only fallen behind schedule once."

All that happened back in the 1870s. As the story goes, Ida married and moved away from the valley. Railroad history has no more details of her life, but it is believed that Ida Hewitt was the first woman locomotive engineer in the United States.

INTO THE TWENTIETH CENTURY

SARAH CLARK KIDDER: SHORT LINE RAILROAD PRESIDENT

Sarah Clark was living with her family on a farm in Forest Grove, Oregon, when she met and married John Kidder in 1870. After the wedding, the bride and groom moved to Grass Valley, California, and built a large house in the lush valley near Nevada City.

Sarah tended a beautiful flower garden, which surrounded a splendid water fountain in the front yard. She hostessed teas, volunteered for an orphan aid society, and looked after a daughter, Beatrice. Sarah especially liked sewing lacy dresses for herself and Beatrice, dresses that were very much the style of the time.

Meanwhile, her husband, who had begun work in Grass Valley as superintendent on a new railroad, bought out the owners and became president of the company. The railroad was called the Nevada County Narrow Gauge. It was a short line that hauled lumber and farm produce. Mainly, it carried gold ore, destined for the United States mint in San Francisco. The line ran twenty-two miles from Nevada City to Colfax—up steep grades, around sweeping curves, over four high trestles, and through tunnels at the gold rush towns of You Bet and Town Talk.

Soon the Nevada County Narrow Gauge was not only carrying freight but passengers, especially families who liked riding out to a park and picnic grounds. For years, John boasted of an excellent record, with few accidents and no robberies on the line. The worst incidents were a bridge fire and the derailment of a circus train.

All seemed to be going well, when John took ill and died. He left his shares of controlling stock to Sarah, thus passing control of the company into her hands. No woman had ever been in such a position in the railroad business before, and whether or not the board of directors eagerly agreed to accept her is not known.

But early in 1901, board members voted Sarah Clark Kidder as president of the Nevada County Narrow Gauge. This made her one of the country's earliest women to head a railroad company.

Sarah left the technical details to a manager, while she took over the business of finance. Certainly, she expected to face problems, as in all businesses, but the first came as a shock. She found out that the company had gone into debt.

How could she deal with a situation like that? she wondered. After all, as a child she had known only life on a farm, and in her married years she had been a wife and homemaker. What business experience did she have?

But Sarah overcame the blow and set out immediately to tackle the problem. First, she needed to pay off the debt. Then, she had to move the company forward by earning higher profits. The most important action she took was to create new business by encouraging additional freight and passenger travel. From all reports, she was praised for doing a remarkable job in accomplishing her goals. In fact, by the end of 1903, hardly three years after her presidency began, the company's annual report showed its best profit in its twenty-seven-year history.

In addition to having financial control, Sarah oversaw improvements on much of the rolling stock that traveled the rails as well as made certain that equipment was repaired and updated.

In 1906, a team of railway inspectors came to Grass Valley for an annual inspection. They reported that there was trouble at Bear River. The trestle was beginning to decay. The team recommended that a new trestle be built farther downstream than its present location so that the trains could cross the river at a higher elevation. This would save the expense of grading and fuel, as well as shorten the distance and running time.

Sarah considered the matter long and hard. Could the company raise enough money to afford a new trestle? Should they rebuild the old one? What would the difference in cost be? Some board members favored building anew. Others said *no*. Finally, Sarah decided that a new trestle was the wisest choice.

But how was she going to raise money to get started? She traveled to San Francisco, discussed the project with bankers, and won their approval for loans. That was bold action for a woman at that time. Because of her leadership, a new trestle of advanced design was built, and when it opened in 1908, it was hailed a great success.

Sarah Clark Kidder worked as the company's president for twelve years, after which she retired and moved to San Francisco, satisfied with all that she had accomplished. Sarah told a newspaper reporter there that being a railroad president certainly was "an unusual position for a woman to fill, but circumstances left me no alternative. It was my husband's desire that I should succeed him."[1]

But she added that she enjoyed her work. "Not only do I know about trimming beautiful dress and home fabrics like voile and Chantilly lace," she said, "but now I also know all about the trim of a locomotive—valve stem brackets, eccentric straps, connecting rods, cylinders, crankshafts, hexagonal nuts, indicators, and piston rods."

MARY PENNINGTON: REFRIGERATOR CAR DESIGNER

It was a hot summer afternoon in 1884. Twelve-year-old Mary Pennington was reading on the veranda of her brick house in Philadelphia, Pennsylvania. Usually she enjoyed stories, but that day she started reading a chemistry book she had found open in her father's library.

Mary was in the middle of a chapter on oxygen and nitrogen when she was struck with fascination about those two chemical elements. "Suddenly I realized that even though oxygen and nitrogen had no color, taste, or odor, they really existed," Mary remembered years later. The subject of chemistry engaged her so thoroughly that she called that moment of discovery a "milestone" in her life.[2]

She decided to study chemistry, although it was rare for women in those days to receive education beyond basic reading, arithmetic, sewing, and proper manners taught at a school for young ladies.

Despite this, after graduating from a young ladies' school, one day Mary boldly walked into the office of a dean at the University of Pennsylvania in Philadelphia and announced that she wished to enroll in the science department.

The dean paused. Then, to Mary's surprise, he gave his consent. When Mary told her parents, they were shocked. Finally, however, they came to accept the idea, and they gave their daughter full support.

Mary finished all her classes toward a degree, but the university board of trustees refused to grant her one because she was a woman. Her professors, however, declared her a special case and awarded her an advanced Ph.D. degree anyway. Afterward, in 1895, she enrolled at Yale University and studied biological chemistry.

Dr. Mary Pennington then went to work as a bacteriologist. That was at the turn of the century, a time when people often got sick or died from impure milk because there were no laws to ensure sanitary conditions in dairies. Not even ice cream that was sold to children from sidewalk pushcarts was safe!

In laboratories and dairies, Mary tested bacteria toxicity levels and regulated temperature controls in milk processing and storage. Her results and guidelines helped promote the earliest laws that improved the quality and safety of milk production throughout the country.

Later, Mary was hired by the U.S. Department of Agriculture, where she supervised fifty-five men in experiments with fish and poultry skinning, scaling, packing, and deep-freezing methods. Her work there became the basis for further improved health standards.

Mary then turned her attention to a problem on the railroads— keeping perishable foods fresh on refrigerator cars. Rails were the link between the nation's farms and its people. And the people liked variety when they sat down to eat. They wanted fresh meats, poultry, and fish, firm fruit, and crisp salads. But how long could such food last as it rolled across the country before the lettuce wilted and the meat turned to rot?

Railroads called refrigerator cars "reefers." The earliest ones were designed with air ventilation openings for cooling. Then came compartments that were filled and refilled with ice, which was better than air ventilation as a coolant, but still not wholly satisfactory.

How was this kind of puzzle to be solved? Certainly not in a laboratory! There was only one thing for Mary to do. She climbed aboard a train, set up equipment in a test car that was coupled between a reefer and the caboose, and rode the rails tens of thousands of miles. Using gauges that determined temperature and humidity, she tested foods under all kinds of conditions and in all kinds of weather—from winters in Maine to scorching summers in the Imperial Valley of California. She investigated ice bunkers, insulation, temperature control, food packing, loading, and warehousing.

In particular, she noted that insulation was too thin, and cracks in the cars caused the insulation to loosen altogether. The most dangerous condition of all, she reported, came from water that dripped on the floors. In that water and in the moist air above, bacteria grew and settled on the foods. Some of that bacteria caused deadly illnesses.

Mary redesigned reefers with added insulation in ice bunkers, walls, floors, and racks. She also designed a forced-air system to give maximum air circulation throughout each car. This was the best solution for that time, and new reefers were a marked improvement for railroad food preservation and for the health and safety of the American people. But for years, railroad officials stubbornly resisted making the suggested changes. Changes would cost money, and they didn't want to spend any more than necessary. Mary fought long and hard until she finally convinced railroad owners to take the right action.

Through her continued work, Dr. Mary Pennington set standards that helped direct food processing, refrigeration, and storage methods. Her standards and regulations governed much of the United States food industry for years to come.

After she retired, she filled her home freezer with frozen foods and served guests tasty dinners of fish, meat, and vegetables. For dessert, she always offered dishes of cold, refreshing—and safe to eat—ice cream.

HARVEY GIRLS ON THE ATCHISON, TOPEKA & SANTA FE

"Young women of good character, attractive, and intelligent,
18 to 30, to work in Harvey Eating Houses in the West"

Young women from all over the country flocked to respond to this advertisement, which first appeared in newspapers in 1883 and ran for years afterward. Those women who met the requirements and passed the training period were hired as waitresses to serve passengers at restaurants built in towns and cities along the Atchison, Topeka & Santa Fe Railway. The waitresses were diligent and dignified in their positions. They were called the Harvey Girls.

Some of the young women became Harvey Girls so they could "see the world." Hazel Williams was only fifteen, but she lied about her age in order to get hired because she was so eager for "a taste of independence."

Ida Stevens,[3] who was eighteen, lived in the small town of Garnett, Kansas, working at a produce company, inspecting chickens. Ida didn't see an advertisement, but one day in 1928 she heard that two women had left town and gotten jobs far beyond Garnett. When Ida learned about their jobs as Harvey Girls, which offered both travel opportunities and good wages, she sent for an application and was hired by mail.

For the first time in her life, Ida boarded a train. And off she traveled to a hotel restaurant in Wellington, Kansas, one hundred fifty miles away. After a few months waitressing in a coffee shop there, she was transferred to a beautiful new hotel in the city of Albuquerque, New Mexico. That was the start of a rewarding career lasting eight years.

Many young women became Harvey Girls because their families

Ida leaves home for the first time to go to Wellington, Kansas, for training as a Harvey Girl. IDA STEVENS PETERSEN COLLECTION

21

needed the money. Bertha Spears's family struggled to make ends meet on their small Oklahoma farm. But no matter how hard they worked, the farm never yielded enough crops to support the lot of them. Bertha quit school and found work as a housekeeper in a distant town and later at a hospital for tuberculosis patients. Meanwhile, Bertha's mother died, and "things went from bad to worse." Finally, the family gave up the farm and hired themselves out as extra hands to another farmer.[4]

Then Bertha met the farmer's daughter, Audrey. She was the most glamorous person Bertha had ever seen. Audrey was a Harvey Girl. Bertha, tired of drudgery and failure, rode off to become a Harvey Girl, too.

Before the Harvey restaurants came into existence, traveling out West was only for the toughest and most stouthearted. The nation's first railroads had been built in the populated north eastern states, and when they started expanding across uncharted western territories, they ventured into rugged land. The Atchison, Topeka & Santa Fe, called simply the Santa Fe, was one of the largest western railway companies. Its main lines ran from Chicago, Illinois, out to the California coast and south through Texas to the Gulf of Mexico.

The earliest travelers crossed wide-open prairies and long stretches of desert without a decent place to stay overnight and with little to eat or drink for days at a time. Sometimes at a stop, men got off a train and hunted a meal of rabbit or even buffalo. And often, water was served at station stops—if passengers didn't mind drinking from the same cup! But that hardly satisfied a hungry stomach or quenched a parched throat.

Small eateries opened up along the route, though they didn't help much. At each stop of ten or twenty minutes, passengers had to make a mad dash to grab a mouthful or two before the train lurched forward and moved on. And what grub those eateries served! Cold, tough meat, greasy eggs, rancid salt pork and beans slung by lumberjacks or cowhands, coffee that looked like dishwater, biscuits that were so hard they were called sinkers.

Then along came Fred Harvey, a stylish Englishman. He made a business arrangement with the Santa Fe, which agreed to let him open and operate restaurants and hotels for the company. He began with a clean, freshly painted ten-seat lunch counter in the railroad's Topeka, Kansas, depot. He served good food and offered speedy, courteous service. Customers were delighted. After that, he opened a little hotel further along the line in Florence, population one hundred. He fixed it up, furnished it with attractive furniture, silver, crystal, and Irish linens, and decorated it with flowers shipped in from the East. Soon Fred Harvey and the Santa Fe expanded to cities in New Mexico, Arizona, and California, using depots and restored boxcars for restaurants, before he started building restaurants and hotels with the Santa Fe's approval.

It was not easy getting fresh foods to the desert locations. The costs of special refrigerator-car shipping were high. But Harvey was willing to pay the price because he insisted on the best. When he found it impossible to keep milk, cream, and eggs fresh, he built dairy farms in the territories so he could get supplies direct.

If you were a Fred Harvey customer, you could eat a lunch of fresh shrimp or veal loaf with mushroom sauce for seventy-five cents or a ham, sardine, and lettuce sandwich for forty-five cents. For dinner you might choose Long Island duckling with compote of apple, French mutton chop grill, or a medallion of poached

Harvey Girls worked long, hard hours. Not a minute on the job could be wasted. When Laura White was assigned to the restaurant in Ash Fork, Arizona, she learned to serve complete meals to sixteen people in twenty-five minutes. She was also required to keep the silverware and china polished. There were to be no frayed napkins, nicked cups, or broken toothpicks. One woman, who served and cooked, learned discipline from her first day on the job when she broke an egg yolk. She was required to start over until she got an egg poached just right for a customer. She was especially nervous, too, because the man had to get to work on time and he was a railroad timekeeper.

The rules and requirements were strict, but the results helped

Love often blossomed in Harvey House coffee shops and restaurants.
KANSAS STATE HISTORICAL SOCIETY

to make the Fred Harvey establishments a success from the first lunch counter in 1876 until many years after Harvey's death in 1901. The business peaked at forty-seven restaurants, fifteen hotels, and thirty railroad dining cars.

The Harvey Girls were not only vital to the success of the Harvey and Santa Fe empires but were also considered to be women who "civilized the wild West" and its brawling, drinking, and gambling men. Fred Harvey was known to tell the men firmly: "Ladies are here. No swearing or foul language. And put up your guns!"

Throughout the years, about a hundred thousand Harvey Girls served Santa Fe customers. Some worked a few years, others advanced their education after they quit. Many made a career of railroad food service. One called the experience so interesting, it was "just like getting an education." About twenty thousand of them married men they met out West—railroadmen, ranchers, cowhands, miners, and customers.

Fred Harvey was an inspired business entrepreneur, but it was the Harvey Girls who really helped his empire flourish.

MARY COLTER: ARCHITECT AND DESIGNER

When Mary Elizabeth Jane Colter was eight years old, she received a gift that was to become her "most valued possession." It was given to her by a family relation, a soldier stationed in the Montana territory after the Battle of the Little Bighorn. He had befriended a group of Northern Cheyenne Indians interned at the army fort. The gift was a sheaf of drawings they had made of animals like deer and buffalo, and human figures, such as a man on horseback and women dancing.[6] Mary treasured the intriguing sketches and looked at them again and again.

Three years later, her family moved from the East Coast to the mill town of St. Paul, Minnesota, and Mary packed her gift carefully for the journey.

In 1880, the population in the St. Paul region was a mixture of settlers and Native American Sioux Indians. Not long after the Colters arrived, a smallpox epidemic swept through the Sioux community. People then knew little about the devastating disease, and fearful of its wider spread, they could only think to burn everything associated with the early victims. Mary's mother tossed all the Indian articles in the house into a fire. But Mary couldn't bear to part with her precious drawings and hid them under her mattress.

Throughout her early school years, Mary grew to deeply appreciate and enjoy art. She devoted herself to classes in drawing, clay modeling, and basket weaving, unusual courses for public schools to offer. After high school, she wanted to continue her education. However, her father died suddenly, leaving Mary, her mother, and sister with little financial support.

Despite this, Mary pleaded to attend an advanced art school. She promised that afterward she would help out by earning money as an art teacher. Finally, her mother agreed, and at the age of seventeen Mary enrolled in a design school in San Francisco, California. There she studied both art and architecture and worked part-time for an architecture firm, an extraordinary job for a woman at that time.

After her graduation, she returned home and spent more than a decade as a teacher, including instructing all-male high school classes in freehand and mechanical drawing. During her vacations, she studied history and archeology at the University of Minnesota.

In the summer of 1901, Mary visited a friend in San Francisco, who introduced her to a man employed by the Fred Harvey Company. Mary told him about her interest in Indian art and mentioned that she would like to try working in the Southwest.

She had almost forgotten that conversation, when the next summer she received a telegram, offering her a job in Albuquerque, New Mexico. She was hired as interior decorator for a new handicrafts gift shop at a Spanish mission–style Harvey Company and Santa Fe Railway hotel, the Alvarado. There she arranged a colorful display of Indian blankets, rugs, pottery, and jewelry. The decor was so attractive that hotel guests and railroad passengers flocked to buy the Indian-made crafts.

Then Mary came up with a worthy idea, sure to attract even more customers. She saw that Indian women and men were working at their crafts on surrounding hotel grounds. Why not invite them inside so guests could watch them engaged in their unique artistic skills? Soon Navajo artisans sat in the shop, weaving blankets in geometric patterns and creating splendid silver and copper jewelry. Business was better than ever for the Navajo artisans, the Fred Harvey Company, and the Santa Fe Railway.

Mary Colter had a fine knowledge of art, and especially appreciated Indian art and culture. Now she was living on land blessed with great natural wonders, like the Grand Canyon and the painted desert. Soon, she came to embrace a philosophy of architecture that would guide her throughout her years as a designer of many exceptional buildings for the Harvey Company and the railroad.

Mary believed that architecture should "grow out of the land," that dwellings should be created in harmony with the surrounding nature. During that time, many architects of the United States were copying and reproducing European styles. But Mary

Designed by Mary Colter as a re-creation of ancient Indian watchtowers, The Watchtower was a Harvey gift shop, rest stop, and viewing site along the south rim of the Grand Canyon.
SHIRLEY BURMAN PHOTOGRAPHER

The ground floor of Mary Colter's Watchtower was called the Kiva, patterned after traditional Indian kiva chambers used for men's religious and social activities.
SHIRLEY BURMAN COLLECTION

did not care about following trends. One writer said that Mary was far "more interested in rediscovering the cultural heritage of the region than in imitating European styles" as other Americans were doing.[7]

At the Grand Canyon in Arizona, Mary designed an Indian arts building, Hopi House. Working with Hopi Indians, she used native

30

Mary Colter hired a Hopi artist to paint the traditional scenes in the Hopi Room. The central scene is the Snake Legend, illustrating the origin of the Snake Dances and the navigation of the Colorado River.
SHIRLEY BURMAN COLLECTION

The Hopi House had a museum space for the Harvey Company's Indian blanket collection, a sales room for local native arts, and a space for artisans to demonstrate their particular skills for visitors.
SHIRLEY BURMAN COLLECTION

stone and wood to "recreate the distinctive dwelling of an ancient culture and to acquaint the public with the richness and beauty of Native American art."[8] The interior was completed with a fireplace, log-beamed ceilings, leather benches and chests, and sand paintings.

At La Fonda hotel in Santa Fe, near the historic pioneer Santa

Mary Colter (right) and Mrs. Harold Ickes, wife of the U. S. Secretary of the Interior, review blueprints for the Bright Angel Lodge on the Grand Canyon rim. GRAND CANYON NATIONAL PARK HISTORICAL SOCIETY

Fe Trail, Mary created a Mexican-style atmosphere. She came up with a unique idea for a hotel. She decorated each room differently. One guest traveler might sleep in a room with a bullfight motif, another in a room with a cowboy or a prairie theme.

Once, after she completed building an "old-looking" dwelling of timber and boulders surrounded by twisted tree stumps, some railroad men teased Mary. "It's dingy and full of cobwebs," one said. "Why don't you clean up this place?" Mary laughed. "You can't imagine what it cost to make it look this old!"

Of all the hotels, depots, and shops that Mary designed and decorated, her favorite was La Posada, the railway station hotel at Winslow, Arizona. This time, she was architect, interior designer, *and* landscaper. La Posada was a sprawling Spanish-style ranch building, with patio, fountain, sunken garden, statues, and a wishing well, all surrounded by acres of orchards. The interior, with arched windows, painted glass panes, engravings, and iron lamps—along with a mixture of Spanish and Chinese art—was elegant. *La Posada* means "the resting place." Santa Fe travelers found Mary's hotel an extraordinary place to rest and enjoy.

Mary also designed china and silverware for the Santa Fe Super Chief dining cars.

She made it possible for millions of rail travelers to take pleasure in their journeys across the Southwest. Her passion for Indian art and culture helped bring to multitudes an understanding of Native Americans and their valuable contributions to the nation.

Mary Elizabeth Jane Colter saved her cherished gift of drawings throughout her life, and upon her death at the age of eighty-eight, she bequeathed the drawings to the Little Bighorn Battlefield National Monument in Montana. It was her wish to return her treasure to the land of the Northern Cheyenne Indians.

WORLD WAR I

DOING THE MEN'S WORK

Late one night in November 1917, Anna Belle Glenn received a message to report immediately to the Frisco lines rail yard in Hugo, Oklahoma. She was working in Fort Smith, Arkansas, as a car distributor, identifying and overseeing rail cars designated to be coupled, or hooked up, to specific trains before they moved out of the yard. The message gave no explanation for the transfer. Sudden changes like that weren't unusual for railroaders, and Anna Belle answered the call at once.

At Hugo, she was sent to a train dispatcher, Mike Brennan. He was in the tower writing up traffic control orders for Frisco line rolling stock, which moved over 480 miles of track.

"You are going to replace a dispatcher," Mike told Anna Belle.

"Me? Dispatch trains?" Anna Belle exclaimed. "I've never done that in my life!" A dispatcher was responsible for lives, as well as for millions of dollars' worth of property! Anna Belle had not heard of a woman being given such a critical and authoritative job.

"There's a war on, you know," Mike said. "The other man here just enlisted. You have his job now."

Mike gave Anna Belle a few instructions, a handful of schedule sheets, and a precision railroad watch. Then he went to eat his supper. Anna Belle was left alone to learn on the job.

Where should she start? she asked herself. How could she know the locations of the trains if she couldn't see them? How did she authorize a train movement order? But this was no time to freeze with fear. Taking a deep breath, she began reading the schedule sheets.

Only minutes later, a message came over the telegraph. Anna Belle had learned the Morse code from her father. Swiftly, she took down the incoming message, a report verifying that a specified train had safely passed a station. Anna Belle logged the train's progress and forwarded the information to stations farther along the line.

Suddenly, another message came in. An operator wanted to know what to do about a late passenger train. It was up to Anna Belle to decide and answer. She was the dispatcher now. Hurriedly, she checked the schedule of trains moving on that section of track. She had to redirect the late train. If not, there would be a "cornfield meet," a head-on collision. And she would be responsible!

At once, Anna Belle dispatched the late train to run onto a siding track. That would allow the on-schedule train to proceed. The receiving operator copied the order and issued it without delay. All was clear. Anna Belle found herself in a sweat, but at the same time she felt excited at having actually put out a train order.

Although telephones were just coming into use for dispatching (automated control panels remained years in the future), dispatchers still depended on the telegraph. Meanwhile, Anna Belle Glenn learned her new job well. "It was sprung on me as a surprise," she said, "but I grew to find the work fascinating and to like it very much."

Seven months earlier, President Woodrow Wilson had appeared before the U.S. Congress. War was raging in Europe, and although America had hoped to remain neutral, Germany, the aggressor, was engaging in submarine warfare, which took American lives at sea. Congress voted to take action, and the president declared war on Germany and the other Central Powers. On April 2, 1917, the United States entered World War I.

The war required mobilization of millions of men. This left a major shortage of labor in the United States. There weren't enough people to produce munitions or to run the railroads needed for transporting the troops and their supplies. This threw the railroads into confusion and chaos. The only way to bring order and to expedite transportation was for the government to take strict, centralized control. This had never happened before in American history. But the nation was in the midst of a wartime emergency, so the government created the U.S. Railroad Administration and nationalized the railroad system.

Thousands of women began to fill the vacancies left in railroad offices, stations, machine shops, rail yards, and roundhouses, where locomotives were kept. They weren't, however, recruited to replace the men who operated the locomotives or worked on the cars while they were moving. Many of the women had been employed in industrial labor in factories or shops that required machine work. Others had been working in traditional "women's sphere" occupations, such as in hotels, restaurants, or textile

This train dispatcher trainee is studying a lineup of railcars and locomotives, learning how they would be switched around in the rail yard.
NATIONAL ARCHIVES

mills. Then, too, there were many who entered the workforce for the first time.

A war emergency aroused strong patriotism, and railroad women proudly went to the aid of the nation. They welcomed the new opportunities at important jobs that offered steady

37

employment and good wages, especially since many sought jobs for economic reasons because male wage earners were now overseas. Salary for a forty-eight-hour workweek averaged ninety-five dollars a month, although reports show that often women were listed as "helpers" and paid less than men for the same tasks. Women enjoyed a new sense of dignity their work offered.

Women worked in engine houses and did mechanical tasks such as inspecting wheel rods for cracks, refueling the tenders, putting sand in the sand dome, and watering locomotives. NATIONAL ARCHIVES

Historian Maurine Greenwald studied and wrote about women and the railroad business during this time. She found that by October 1, 1918, near the war's end, 101,785 women were employed. Most, by far, were workers like clerks, typists, stenographers, and ticket sellers. The second largest group worked in roundhouses and yards, mostly in traditional roles of cleaning and maintenance. The next largest group was employed in personal services like kitchen, laundry, and nursing. Telegraphers accounted for the fourth group. Last, some five thousand women gained both skilled and unskilled jobs in shop production. They checked freight house inventory and operated turntables—huge round platforms at the end of a track line, on which locomotives are turned. They worked heavy tool equipment, cutting metals with an oxyacetylene cutter, forging metal parts with drill presses or steam hammers, or welding metal sections together by torch heat. They also cleaned, repaired, and tested this machinery.

In the B & O's Mt. Clare shops in Baltimore, Maryland, twenty women labored at heavy jobs. After the war, nineteen left for other work or to return home. But one, Amy Fisher, remained in the forge shop through World War II and for several years beyond.

She operated a steam hammer, a gigantic power-driven tool used to shape metal. Steam hammers weigh from one hundred pounds to several tons and can be operated either to fall with crushing force or to break a nutshell without touching the nut inside. People who worked with Amy agreed that her hand coordination was so exact they would entrust her with their pocket watches. She could bring the giant hammerhead right down to tap the crystal without causing a crack!

Black women experienced further discrimination yet. In general, they replaced the white women who had moved into positions left vacant by men. Now black women operated elevators, waitressed in cafés, and worked in textile mills or at other clothing manufacturing jobs. On the railroad, they were hired in roundhouses and yards. At first, they appeared to be advancing, and they raised their hopes. But black women faced the same biases as they had in the past. They were hired only to clean, move supplies, transfer freight, and sort soiled laundry. No matter how well they performed, and no matter how highly they were praised, it was almost impossible for them to win promotions.

Most railroad women dressed fashionably, but these New York Railway conductors wore military-like uniforms of pants, leggings, and trench coats. This "male" appearance was commonly encountered during World War I employment. NATIONAL ARCHIVES

With more and more women added to payrolls, entirely new positions were created to look after their needs and benefits. The Santa Fe hired three women as service inspectors, who arranged to make facilities like toilets, rest rooms, and convenient lodgings available for female employees. For women who worked in remote areas, boxcars were freshly painted and comfortably furnished to serve as their homes.

As rail companies created small service departments, the U.S. Railroad Administration formed the Women's Service Section (WSS), appointing as its manager an industrial social worker named Pauline Goldmark. The WSS assisted women nationwide by promoting comfortable, safe work conditions for them and by

In rural areas of New York State, the New York Central Railroad hired local farm women for depot yard maintenance. JEFFREY MOREAU COLLECTION

offering support to those who registered harassment complaints. The WSS also advocated equal pay and promotions.

One woman, Ella Barnett, had worked her way up on the New York Central, until she rose to chief clerk in the return-ticket department. But the company listed her only as helper, which meant that they could pay her less than a male. The WSS helped get her proper listing on the payroll and, finally, the salary she deserved.

Pauline Goldmark admitted that the WSS often found itself in a dilemma. "It was difficult to stand for women's rights," she said, "and also have to stand for their protection at the same time."

A supervisor, Mrs. G. A. Reilly, believed that "someday women will achieve success in the railroad industry in proportion to their vision and ability." But in the meanwhile, she recognized that "women are still on trial and are subjected to stricter discipline than men." Because of this, she felt obligated to give women "friendly advice," to help deflect criticism.

"Are you on time?" she asked them. "Are you really sick when you so report? Are you in the habit of going to the drugstore to telephone during business hours?" And on the subject of dress, she said, "When you come to work, you are not going to a Mardi Gras party where cosmetics and abbreviated skirts are permissible. The style of dress reflects upon a woman's intelligence." She offered an important reminder, too. "Women will not suc ceed by emulating the inefficient businessmen, but by proving that a first-class woman is better than a second-class man."[3]

At the war's end, on November 11, 1918, men returned to their jobs back home, and women faced losing theirs. Many officials were glad to let women go, sometimes dismissing them at a moment's notice on unfair pretenses. Woman after woman was suddenly reported to have "used bad language," "gotten drunk," or "distracted men at work by wearing short skirts." A good number of women were allowed to remain, but they continued mostly in traditional domestic jobs. Historian Maurine Greenwald found that women lost ground in the areas of nontraditional railroad work. Several historians believed that railroad women had made remarkable advances by the end of the war. Maurine Greenwald, however, disagreed. While women made some lasting gains, she concluded in her study, negative attitudes toward their working on the railroad had not changed much at all.

A group of men on the Pennsylvania Railroad wrote a letter to their supervisor. "Our men came first before the war, why not now? We will say the female help was kind to help men out, but having them two years is two years too long." And they wrote—unfairly, because it was not true—that women worked only to buy luxuries like clothes and jewelry, "spend[ing] all they make to put on their backs."[4]

As women made important contributions to the wartime economy, they took some steps forward and some steps back. In the end, they learned a great deal about their own strengths and resolve. They showed how highly capable and spirited they could be.

Olive Dennis
Research Engineer

When Olive Dennis was growing up in Baltimore, Maryland, her mother urged her to sew, cook, and play with dolls. But no matter how hard Olive tried to please her mother, she preferred watching builders on construction sites. She was far happier building a dollhouse than playing with dolls.

When she was eleven, her father dismantled an old woodshed out in the family's backyard and allowed her to use the lumber. She measured and sawed and pounded, building a playhouse, one that was actually big enough to enter.

It was no surprise, then, that Olive decided on a career in structural engineering. Her studies began with math and science at Goucher College in Maryland and continued at Columbia University in New York City. She earned a degree in civil engineering at Cornell University in 1920.

People asked her, "What can you, a woman, do as an engineer?" Olive resented the question because she believed that she, as well as other women, was qualified to work in many capacities.

Eventually, she was hired by the Baltimore & Ohio Railroad as a draftsman to design bridges. Drafting had not been her goal, but after spending so many years in school, she welcomed the opportunity to

Olive Dennis designed commemorative dishes for the one hundredth anniversary of the Baltimore & Ohio Railroad. SHIRLEY BURMAN COLLECTION

apply the theories she had studied to concrete and steel construction.

A year later, the B & O president came to her with an idea for a new job especially for a woman. Nearly half the passengers were women, he said, and he wanted to find ways to make their travel more enjoyable. He knew that Olive had technical training and, of course, she also had a woman's point of view, which would allow her to understand and analyze women's needs. The new position he offered her was called Engineer of Service.

"This was not the sort of job I had dreamed of either," Olive said. But it sounded intriguing. At once, she put all her knowledge, technical training, and energy into the new "woman's job." In the first year, she traveled forty thousand miles as a passenger, interviewing hundreds of other passengers and observing everything possible, from ventilation and lighting to seats, flooring, rest rooms, dining cars, and menus.

As a result of her investigations, she created a new ventilation system; nonglare ceiling lights that could be dimmed at night; interiors with attractive, restful colors like sea green and mulberry; and reclining, contoured seats with adjustable footrests. She also installed spacious rest rooms with tiled floors that were more sanitary and durable than the linoleum used earlier, and rest room facilities for women with babies. And for women who requested them, she arranged for light meals to be served in the dining cars.

Olive enjoyed her work so much that she remained as engineer of service with the company throughout her career. Later, when rail coaches began losing out to increased air travel, the B & O came up with a bold, new concept to boost business. It was the luxurious,

Olive Dennis reviews blueprints and sorts through a stack of upholstery swatches for the Cincinnatian, *a fast new luxurious train that had its inaugural run in January 1947.* BALTIMORE & OHIO RAILROAD MUSEUM, WATKINS RESERVE LIBRARY

streamlined train the Cincinnatian, which raced from Baltimore to Cincinnati, Ohio, in record-breaking time. Olive helped design every aspect of the new train, from the sleek, blue exterior to the colorful, comfortable designs and structures inside. The Cincinnatian continued a trend toward luxury travel that also included newly designed trains for commuters. Not only was Olive Dennis an engineer with "a woman's point of view," but she stood at the forefront in combining keen imagination with new and innovative methods of industrial research.

Part of the streamliner era, the Cincinnatian's steam locomotive had a metal shroud cover over most of the engine's moving parts. BALTIMORE & OHIO RAILROAD MUSEUM, WATKINS RESERVE LIBRARY

NURSES AND HOSTESSES
ON BOARD

A Union Pacific passenger train destined for Los Angeles was hurtling over the steel rails late one winter night in 1939. Shortly before two o'clock in the morning, when the train was just outside of Las Vegas, Nevada, the crew received a message that they couldn't make it through to Los Angeles. Severe rainstorms had caused flooding in wide areas of California, and much of the Union Pacific's tracks were washed out.

At the Las Vegas station, the passengers were awakened and evacuated from the train. Then they were transferred onto buses, which were to take them to their final destination.

Fortunately for the travelers, there were two other people on board—Ruth Morgan and Mildred Nims—stewardess-nurses, who worked for the railroad, taking care of passengers' varied personal and medical needs. In that middle of the night emergency, they faced the daunting job of assisting dozens of evacuees.

The most urgent task during the transfer was helping mothers traveling with babies and young children. The two women had to prepare sterilized bottles and enough canned milk formula to last for many hours, since buses didn't have kitchens as trains did.

Four buses were put into service, but, of course, Ruth and Mildred couldn't assist on all of them at once. At every rest stop, they hurried back and forth from one bus to the other, to help as much as possible.

Not long after the buses had set out, it was discovered that the babies' milk, which had been poured into thermoses to keep warm, had turned sour. No babies became ill, but with nothing to drink, one infant after another started fussing and crying. Fresh milk was needed as soon as possible. It wasn't easy to find an open restaurant, but they finally did, and the stewardess-nurses bought enough milk to satisfy all immediate needs.

When the buses arrived in Los Angeles the next day, Ruth and Mildred were exhausted and disheveled, but triumphant in their jobs.[1]

Stewardess-nursing was part of a new field of employment called *industrial nursing*. The Union Pacific Railroad introduced it in 1935, a time when the nation was struggling desperately to recover from a serious economic downturn known as the Great Depression. Businesses and banks closed. Farm prices fell. Millions of people were unemployed. Companies grappling to survive looked for innovative ways to attract new customers. Railroads, with less freight to ship and fewer people who could afford to travel, also needed to find new ways to create business.

The Union Pacific came up with the idea of encouraging travel by promoting personal, specialized care aboard their cars. If a family couldn't afford a trip, a child could be sent alone on the train and be assured of supervision by a licensed registered nurse. If an elderly or disabled person hesitated to make a journey, he or she was promised individual assistance from departure to arrival. First-aid treatment was available, as was assistance for mothers with babies.

Santa Fe courier-nurse Katherine Anderson finds time to show her young passengers how to play games and color a book. KANSAS STATE HISTORICAL SOCIETY

Helen Hansmann worked on the Chicago, Burlington & Quincy's new Zephyr trains, among the earliest to use diesel-powered engines instead of steam locomotives. The streamlined Zephyrs ran at such dizzying, record-breaking speeds—more than one hundred miles per hour—that she spent much of her time helping passengers suffering from motion sickness.

Before industrial nursing, the care of passengers en route was entirely in the hands of men. Stewardess-nurses were the first women to work on trains while the trains were in motion. During World War I, tens of thousands of women had been hired by railroads, but those who labored inside the cars or the locomotives worked only while the trains were in a yard or a roundhouse.

The new female attendants were hired mainly because they offered a boost to business. One B & O promotional advertisement noted:

> "We realized that the railroad could never succeed without the goodwill of women travelers. Women are the most loyal friends any business can have."

What better way to win the patronage of those "loyal friends" than to offer them the service of other women who could "help make the train feel more like home"?

Helen Dixon, on the Southern Pacific, called herself a "feminine touch in a typically masculine sphere. Long ago, when women started working in barbershops, men thought that was the height of intrusion. If they had ever thought that someday

In the late 1930s, several railroads came up with a new promotional idea—a Junior Stewardess-Nurse Club for young girls. Applicants received a train primer to study, emphasizing safety, general railroad knowledge, and travel.
SHIRLEY BURMAN COLLECTION

women would become an integral part of a railroad train crew, those old-timers would probably have suffered apoplexy!"[2]

Other railroads followed Union Pacific's lead, but they didn't all require the women to be nurses. Some companies called them hostesses or attendants; others called them couriers or stewardesses. Competition increased. An ad for B & O promised that attendants would "send a telegram for you" and "give you travel information."

The New York Central Empire Girls would "happily take the kiddies on a tour of the train."

The Pullman Company catered to their young passengers with special colorful booklets, games, and coloring books. SHIRLEY BURMAN COLLECTION

A 1937 traveler's brochure advertising stewardess-nurse service. SHIRLEY BURMAN COLLECTION

The Union Pacific reminded people: "Don't confuse hostesses with their more qualified stewardess-nurses."

Whether a nurse or hostess, most were required to be unmarried, not too short or too tall, and within an age range from about twenty-two to thirty-two. It was also necessary to have a "pleasing personality and be well-groomed and well-behaved."

The young women wore uniforms, usually a stylish suit and cap. They slept in sleeping cars on the road and fine hotels while on layover in a city. Salary was about one hundred twenty-five dollars a month, with all expenses paid.

Ruth Morgan, one of the stewardess-nurses on the Union Pacific the night of the train evacuation, had grown up in the prairie town of Blair, Nebraska. As a young girl, she had been fascinated with "bugs, butterflies, and birds." Soon, she came to enjoy caring for people, young and old, and by her high school graduation, she decided on a nursing career.

Following three years of training, Ruth became a licensed registered nurse and worked first as an assistant night supervisor in a city hospital and then as a civilian nurse in a military hospital.

One evening, a friend telephoned to tell her about a newspaper advertisement he had read. The ad urged registered nurses to apply for jobs on the Union Pacific Railroad. At that time, the service had been under way for two years and had been deemed so successful that the railroad was expanding its program.

Ruth liked hospital nursing, but this job was unique. She applied and was accepted. Along with several other registered nurses, she took a short training course in Omaha, Nebraska, from the chief stewardess-nurse, Florette Welp, before making the first of hundreds of journeys.

From the start, and throughout a four-year career on the railroad, Ruth enjoyed taking care of travelers. Sometimes it was routine work, and other times, it was adventurous. Always, she found it rewarding. And always she felt that she was respected and that her services were highly valued by the people she met and assisted.

While many people considered the work important, there were men, and also women, in the industry and in the public who refused to take hostessing seriously. Later, the work even came to be viewed as demeaning to women. But for a time, when women were barred from entering so many fields, working on railroad cars during their operation was clearly a breakthrough.

"We were lucky," Blanche Virgil Hobza said. "We had a salary

Union Pacific's stewardess-nurse Ruth Morgan handles the baby feeding chore while the mother takes a break. UNION PACIFIC MUSEUM COLLECTION

and an expense account during the Depression. We had wonderful opportunities. I loved to travel and didn't miss visiting one state. I think you get riding-the-rails in your blood."[3]

Another woman, Flora Davidson, felt that she was "thoroughly part of modern American life." She found adventure, romance, and a great many interesting people along the way. But above all, she treasured "the personal sense of achievement" that she had gained on the railroad.

On December 7, 1941, Ruth Morgan was working on a train headed for Cheyenne, Wyoming. Some of the cars were filled with military men on their way to their assigned bases. Europe was in the midst of a war, started by Nazi Germany. Even though the United States had not yet entered the war, the railroads were already being used for transporting servicemen and supplies in the event of war.

That day, some soldiers on the train were listening to a radio, when suddenly they heard an announcement. Japan had bombed America's naval base at Pearl Harbor in Hawaii in an early-morning sneak attack. Thousands of men were killed or wounded.

The next day, President Franklin D. Roosevelt would declare war against Japan. (Only days later, Nazi Germany and Italy, who had earlier signed a pact with Japan, would declare war on the United States.)

Meanwhile, news of the attack and talk of imminent war spread throughout the train. "Everyone was speechless," Ruth Morgan remembered. "It was a frightening moment." As soon as the train reached Cheyenne, all the servicemen got off, "orderly, but very emotional," so that they could receive orders from their superiors and begin to mobilize.

A few weeks after America's entry into war, Union Pacific and some of the other companies dismissed their attendants, since

At the outbreak of World War II, Union Pacific's president, William Jeffers, reluctantly said farewell to his railroad's nurses, but not before a group of them posed for a V-for-Victory picture.
RUTH MORGAN WEITKAMP COLLECTION

their services were no longer needed. Routine life on the home-front changed during wartime, and families didn't travel much.

One of those servicemen was a soldier named Norman Weitkamp. He had met and fallen in love with Ruth Morgan and decided to propose marriage to her before he was called into action. Ruth accepted his proposal, and she and Norman were married. After Norman returned from the war, he and Ruth settled in Seattle, Washington, and raised a family.

Decades later, Ruth Morgan Weitkamp looked back at her railroad career and recalled, "It was a marvelous experience. If I could fit into my uniform and find a train, I would do the job all over again."

WORLD WAR II

MAKING THE VICTORY TRAINS RUN

The year was 1942. The United States was at war. The nation's men were fighting overseas. A patriotic young woman from Flushing, New York, Mary Ellen Cookman,[1] wanted to come to the aid of her country, too.

Cookie, as she was called, considered joining the armed forces. But a poster on a railway station wall caught her attention—the message urged women to apply for work on the Pennsylvania Railroad. Within days, she applied and was hired as a passenger-train brakeman.

After a physical exam, a first-aid course, and several weeks of training, Cookie became a qualified railroad worker, wearing a men's-style suit, vest, and tie, Red Cross industrial shoes, and a hairnet.

Her duties were wide and varied. She prepared cars for the passengers and helped them board. She sold, punched, collected, and counted tickets. She also checked brakes, coupled and uncoupled cars, changed hose equipment between cars when they alternated the use of steam and electricity, and signaled warnings, by hand, lantern, or a small explosive cap called a torpedo. When her train was slowed or stopped, Cookie had to walk a distance and clip a torpedo on the track to protect the train. The first approaching train would roll over it, setting off a loud boom and alerting the engineer: *Caution. Proceed at reduced speed.*

By tradition, railroaders who were employed the longest acquired seniority, and they were given the choicest jobs and hours. At first, Cookie was assigned scattered local runs on trains that stopped every few miles, with a shift of sixteen hours on duty and eight off, seven days a week. Finally, the next year, she was moved up to a steady night run on a train dubbed "The Owl," which ran from Pennsylvania Station in New York City to Head Bay Junction, New Jersey. Passengers were mostly factory workers and troops. Many of the servicemen were wounded and in transit home or to a hospital.

"The Owl" was a preferred assignment because it offered a steady schedule. Although the work was still wearying, Cookie liked the job enormously. "I believed we were doing something important during wartime," she said. "I served and worked with people of all races and from all different kinds of backgrounds, and I was impressed at seeing how the country pulled together during those war years."

On September 2, 1945, Japan formally surrendered to the United States. That day was called V-J Day—Victory over Japan. Americans everywhere were out in the streets cheering and celebrating the war's end. Cookie was on duty. During a station stop in Perth Amboy, New Jersey, she was disconnecting an air hose between two cars. In the midst of the excitement going on around her, she got "distracted and careless," and a 250-pound metal nozzlelike device on the hose, called an anglecock, slipped from her hand and landed on her foot, shattering several bones.

With the war ended, servicemen returning to their jobs, and her broken foot in a cast, Cookie decided it was time to quit the railroad and look for work elsewhere.

Many women who worked at jobs like Cookie's quit or were fired when the war was over. But there were some, like Irene Ingison, who stayed on and made a career of railroading.

Irene was a switch tender on the New York Central, working in the Syracuse yard on a sprawling network of tracks. She coupled and uncoupled cars, which then would be pushed by engines onto designated tracks. She also helped maintain and inspect brake equipment, wheels, and air hoses. A leak, a break, or an overheated part, and particularly, overheated friction-bearing wheels called hotboxes, could result in disaster.

Even though every move in the yard was carefully controlled, there were always possibilities for something to go awry, and Irene had to be constantly alert for mishaps or emergencies. "If a rail car was going to wreck or run into something, you didn't care what your duties were," she said. "You'd climb up on a narrow platform behind the car and turn the stiff brake wheel until you got the car slowed down or stopped." On the ground, you might have to throw switches that were "out of whack" or frozen from ice; clean your own switches if maintenance help was low; or jump boxcars, which might land you in a car full of coal.

Irene worked in all kinds of weather, including severe winters, which she admitted were "tough even on an outdoors person like myself." Irene Ingison considered herself a "real railroader," and she stayed with the New York Central for more than thirty years.[2]

When the United States entered World War II, the railroad industry wasn't caught in the chaos it had faced in World War I.

This time, rail companies anticipated the country's needs and demands. They increased production of rolling stock early on and prepared for industry and military cooperation so that the government didn't have to take control of the railroad.

Women were sought from the start and soon were being aggressively recruited. *Victory, the Official Weekly Bulletin of the Office of War Information,* in Washington, D.C., on November 24, 1942, urged railroads to "hire more women, improve training . . . to meet labor shortage." The Office of

It was not an accident that Pennsylvania Railroad chose to use a motherly model as Mrs. Casey Jones in its advertisement. Everyone, including mothers and grandmothers, was expected to help with the war effort. SHIRLEY BURMAN COLLECTION

An all-women crew of locomotive wipers wash, scrub, and polish a Southern Pacific engine at the Bakersfield, California, yard before releasing it for service. SOUTHERN PACIFIC RAILROAD, SHIRLEY BURMAN COLLECTION

Defense Transportation reported that rail companies were "slow to utilize women in many jobs" and called upon them to "accelerate" hiring and training programs. Eventually, in the peak year of 1945, more than 259,000 American women went to work for the railroad industry, several thousand of them in non-traditional jobs.

The Santa Fe employed 3,427 women, 35 percent of whom were assigned to work usually done by men. One issue of the *Santa Fe Magazine* noted that Sally Perez, a mother of three children, who had been a store clerk and had never used a machine before, now operated a drill press in a pipe and tin shop. Gladys Des Jardins was a timekeeper. Juanita Hernandez cleaned roller bearings.

On the Southern Pacific lines, Elizabeth Barnes, wife of a blacksmith, operated an eighteen-hundred-pound steam hammer, while Mabel Anderson, wife of a switchman, filled locomotive fuel oil tanks with heavy, greasy crude oil. Ethel Moore and Della Cramer tended two roaring rivet-heating furnaces in the Brooklyn car repair shop. In Eugene, Oregon, a team of six women, called by co-workers "a mobile gang that was always on the go," added water to locomotive boilers and shoveled cinders. They cleaned and stripped freight cars, pulling up wood strips that had been nailed down to keep freight boxes from shifting.

Safety rules guided women in every company. Southern Pacific listed:

> Coveralls or slacks preferred; no loose sleeves on clothing
> Only low-heel shoes with closed toes permitted
> Hair to be covered with cap, turban, or bandanna
> No jewelry or other ornaments that might get caught in machinery

SHE'S BEEN WORKING ON THE RAILROAD

Goggles to be worn when necessary as they are specified
for men
Gloves to be worn except when they may get caught in
moving machinery
No heavy lifting
Face equipment when descending ladder
No running
Look in both directions when crossing tracks

*Mabel Anderson was one of the many spirited young
women who did not hesitate to help their country in
its time of need after their husbands were called into
the military.* SHIRLEY BURMAN COLLECTION

For the most part, women were gradually becoming accepted. Some 350,000 railroad men had been called to arms in Europe and in the Pacific. "A woman's place has come to be the one where she is most happy and useful," one woman said, "and for many that means a job in industry. Many take care of both jobs [also housewife] and do them well."[3]

Still, it was difficult to overcome the notion that a woman's place was only at home, and industry women continued to confront resentment and harassment in one way or another.

"We were definitely not welcomed by the guys," Mary Ellen Cookman said. "Some of them did everything they could to discourage us." One snowy night, "The Owl" was crossing desolate farmland, and it was ordered onto a siding track to let another train pass. Cookie got out and set up a torpedo signal. After all was clear, and "The Owl" was ready to proceed, the engineer purposely did *not* blow the whistle that by routine told Cookie to get on board again. Suddenly the engineer thrust the train forward, leaving her stranded. She walked over a mile until she found a farmhouse, where a family took her in for the rest of the night. The following day she trekked back and caught "The Owl" as it passed through on its next scheduled run.

Irene Ingison recalled, "When we started, we took a lot of heat. The men played dirty tricks on us. They'd nail my lantern to the floor. They'd put pebbles and toilet paper in my gloves. One evening when I fell asleep, they blackened my face with cork . . .

"There was no powder room for the ladies! Just a men's room with cold water and brown soap . . .

"The engineers resented the women something terrible. A lot of them wouldn't even let us ride on the engine to get from switch to switch—I'd have to walk miles at night sometimes. The older ones wouldn't even talk to me."

Elizabeth Barnes's father was proud of his daughter when she joined the railroad, saying "Elizabeth should make a darn good railroad man!" SOUTHERN PACIFIC RAILROAD, SHIRLEY BURMAN COLLECTION

During the war, many materials were reused or cut up for scrap to be melted down. This laborer uses an acetylene torch to salvage the good parts. SOUTHERN PACIFIC RAILROAD, SHIRLEY BURMAN COLLECTION

Several times Irene went home and cried, vowing never to go back. But after a year, she said, she began to understand that even though some of the men teased her, they also respected the women willing to stick it out.

Men's negative attitudes were often revealed in less direct ways. Company magazines used a condescending tone in describing women as "girls," "the gals," or "the fair sex" and expressed surprise that they were capable and "valiant."

The *Santa Fe Magazine* issue of August 1943 noted that "Eleven colored women are at work in the Galveston shops,

*Moving a heavy set of wheels is made easier with the help of a dolly to
lift the wheels and axle.* BALTIMORE & OHIO RAILROAD MUSEUM

greasing locomotives, serving as sand driers, cleaning coaches
and handling other manual jobs . . . 'Laura Jones is as good a sand
drier as almost any man,' declares A. J. Gay, general foreman."

The *Southern Pacific Bulletin* of November 1942 mused,
"Perhaps it won't be long before we have lace curtains in the
roundhouse."

BROTHERHOOD UNIONS

Railroad men had formed several different unions called brotherhoods, in which they organized to fight for fair and safe working
conditions. But the brotherhoods opposed the admission of

Athabaskan women Gandy dancers working for the Alaska Railroad. The name Gandy *came from the manufacturing firm that built tools for the track workers, while the word* dancers *referred to the foot-stomping dance they did while tamping down the rock ballast around the ties and rails.* ANCHORAGE MUSEUM ARCHIVES, HUGH W. JONES PHOTOGRAPHER women. A spokesman for the Office of Defense Transportation declared that female membership was unnecessary because women "cannot work in all phases of train service . . . And as a matter of fact, it's questionable whether they fit in any part of train service at all." The American Federation of Labor (AFL) Employment Department asserted that in barring women "we are only trying to protect them from very heavy work." Another union, however, allowed that due to a labor shortage, local branches could admit women. But they had to sign a statement agreeing that membership could be withdrawn whenever the union "judged the emergency to cease." Moreover, in the event of accidents, illness, or death, those temporary members were to be denied financial benefits.

It was 1944, and the United States was still at war. Jocelyn Wagner had majored in literature at Columbia University and was working as a receptionist at a movie studio in New York when she "got fired up with wartime patriotism, and the romantic notion of doing a man's job."

After reading a Pennsylvania Railroad ad in the *New York Times*, offering $7.11 a day for unskilled labor with no prior experience, Jocelyn got herself hired out to work the Pennsy's Jersey Coast passenger run. Along with several other women, she was classified as brakeman and trained to survey and inspect brake power on each car. Their duties, though, consisted mostly of passenger conductors' duties—collecting, punching, and sorting tickets; calling out stops; and aiding people coming on board or getting off at the thirty-two stations along the run.

It was not long after she began that Jocelyn realized how complex running a railroad was, with its "staggering lot of logistics" like checking road and equipment conditions, switching cars to different tracks, and locating cars to make up a full train. She realized, too, the complexities that existed among the crew, such as disputes over wage differences, assignments, and seniority entitlements.[4]

One area in which women were treated differently was in organized labor unions. Most of the men belonged to a union, which gave them insurance benefits in case of accident, illness, or death. They also received the right of grievance, allowing them to protest if they believed they were wronged. Of course, when Pennsy women sought to join the lodge of Brotherhood of Railroad Trainmen, they were rejected.

Even after gathering petition signatures of women as well as men who were sympathetic to the cause, they were still refused. They didn't quit, however. Jocelyn went to see the president of the Congress of Industrial Organization's (CIO) Transport Workers Union, who apologized that he couldn't help because he was concerned with organizing smaller railroad unions into one large one. Helping a few females would not move him toward his goal.

Finally, two supportive brotherhood officials paved the way for the Pennsy women to be admitted as "special members for the duration of their employment." Twenty-seven attended their first meeting in a musty, old building in Philadelphia. They were ignored that evening, but that didn't stop them from attending the next meeting and the next.

The determined women persisted, until finally their collective voices were heard. Instead of standing up and speaking only for themselves, they wisely called for improved working conditions and rights for *all* railroad employees. Therefore, men at the meetings were more willing to pay attention because they were likely to get added benefits for themselves.

Before the first year was out, new rulings came down amending the organization's constitution. Women were to receive equal pay for equal work, or at least they were allowed the right to protest if they felt wronged. Membership requirements were changed, as well. Black men had also been refused membership, as was the case in many of the unions. But now this brotherhood's earlier requirement of being a white male was deleted.

Jocelyn Wagner and three other of the most vocal women were recognized as "the first women organizers in the history of the Brotherhood of Railroad Trainmen." Jocelyn recalled, "The old slumberous brotherhood was taking on a new look."

Certainly, times were changing.

Jobs Held by Women During World War II

GENERAL SUPERINTENDENT

TRAIN MASTER AND MASTER MECHANIC
Train Master's Stenographer
Road Master's Clerk

LINE OFFICE JOBS
Agent
Telegraph Operator
Crew Caller
Station Wagon Driver

STATION AND CLERICAL
Ticket Clerk
Reservation Clerk
Cashier
Assistant Steamer Clerk
Timekeeper
Blue Printer
Tabulating Machine Operator
Typewriter Repairman
Freight Loss and Damage
   Investigator

Freight Handler
Tracer
Demurrage (misplaced freight)
  Clerk
Manifest Clerk
Yard Clerk and Train Checker

ENGINE HOUSE AND
ROUNDHOUSE WORKERS
Roundhouse Clerk
Coach Cleaner
Engine Wiper
Cab Cleaner
Washer on Wash Rack
Boiler Washer Helper
Fire Builder
Ash Pit Man
Lubricator Filler
Inside Hostler (car mover)
  Helper
Turntable Operator
Trucker (driver of supplies
  within rail yard)

YARD WORKERS
Car Clerk
Laborer
Track Sweeper
Carman Helper
Hostler

SHOPS
Upholsterer Helper
Locomotive Painter Helper
Blacksmith Shop
Store Supplyman

MECHANICAL DEPARTMENTS
Draftsman
Machinist Helper
Sheet Metal Worker
Steam Hammer Operator
Drill Press Operator
Boilermaker Helper

OPERATING DIVISION
Brakeman
Conductor

ONBOARD SERVICES
Baggageman
Chair Car Attendant (replaced
  porters during diesel era)

COMMUNICATIONS (SIGNALS)
Signalman
Assistant Signalman
Towerman
Crossing Flagman

YESTERDAY, TODAY, AND TOMORROW

BREAKING BARRIERS

Christene Gonzales[1] grasped the throttle in the cab of the two-hundred-ton diesel engine as her train of loaded freight cars thundered over the rails. Christene was an engineer trainee on the Santa Fe Railway, running between Texas and New Mexico. That was the first time she had sat in full control of a locomotive.

Am I really doing this? she asked herself. She was "scared and overwhelmed," but she also felt breathless with excitement. What a tremendous amount of power to hold in her hands!

Streaking forward was one thing. Stopping was something else. A train running at fifty miles an hour on level track needs a mile and a half to come to a complete stop. Now Christene was on a downhill run, and that required even greater control. She steeled herself, thrust the throttle into the idle position, and applied the air brake. The motion of deceleration was forceful. The noise was earsplitting. Finally, the gigantic train came to rest.

Railroading went far back in Christene Gonzales's family.

76

A great-grandfather and a grandfather had worked on the Louisville & Nashville Railroad. A grandmother was once a Harvey Girl. Christene's father was a conductor, and her mother, who had worked as a telegraph operator when she was fifteen, later became the El Paso, Texas, office manager on the Santa Fe.

When Christene was a child in El Paso, she had neither a dream nor a passing thought about a railroad life for herself. She was raising rabbits, a parrot, and a French poodle, and it seemed likely that she might become a veterinarian.

But one day her mother heard that the Santa Fe had agreed to comply with new government regulations calling for equal employment opportunities. That meant the company had to accept applications from women who wanted to operate locomotives or to become hoggers or hogheads, as engineers are called. Mrs. Gonzales passed the news along to her daughter.

Keen on the idea of active, challenging work, Christene applied. Five feet six inches and 120 pounds, she wasn't large or athletic, and she had never used a tool as simple as a screwdriver. But after a series of interviews that showed her to be determined and willing, she was hired as a trainee. A job wasn't guaranteed, however. Following the training period, there would be an evaluation to determine whether or not she would qualify.

In the spring of 1973, Christene started taking locomotive operation instruction classes. Then, as an extremely important part of her training, she rode many hours in the cab with engineers, who always sat on the right-hand side. She learned railroad control signals, which are communicated by means of hand formations, lanterns, engine whistles, and radios. All of these methods are needed because voice signals don't carry over the roar of the engine.

SHE'S BEEN WORKING ON THE RAILROAD

In the 1970s, Christene Gonzales was one of many young women who stepped up into the formerly sacred domain of men—the locomotive cab. SANTA FE RAILWAY

Today, Operation Lifesaver, a public railroad educational safety program, takes up most of Christene Gonzales Aldeis's time, but she has not lost her touch on the throttle.
SHIRLEY BURMAN PHOTOGRAPHER

Christene also observed and assisted in freight train operations and moved locomotives to and from roundhouses. Her instructors agreed that she showed "exceptional ability" at grasping the complex work, and they recommended her for the final stages of preparation.

In the past, engineer training had meant years of apprenticeship first as a fireman. "A man would spend at least twenty years shoveling coal before moving to the right-hand side of the cab," Christene's grandfather said, recalling steam locomotive days, "and only a few of the thousands working toward that goal would make it to that prized seat." But now with diesel engines and new technology, training on many railroads was speeded up by use of a simulator—a large, mechanical device that imitated actual locomotive operations.

After the simulator work, Christene passed a series of written and oral exams. Her scores were excellent. She qualified and became the first woman locomotive engineer on the Santa Fe Railway.

At first, the men asked her, "Why aren't you home washing dishes?" Sometimes they just whispered behind her back, "She won't last long." But Christene Gonzales (now Aldeis) has been an engineer for nearly twenty-five years. "I still feel my heart beating in my throat every time I go out," she says. "I still feel the power and the excitement."

One day in 1979, Linda Niemann[2] saw a Southern Pacific newspaper ad seeking railroad brakemen. Linda held an advanced Ph.D. degree in literature, but she couldn't find a satisfying job that paid a decent salary.

The railroad offered good wages. Besides, in addition to enjoying reading and writing, she also liked the rigorous outdoor life, rock climbing, swimming, and kayaking. She responded to the ad.

Linda was one of three female and fifteen male brakemen hired. Training began with classroom instruction and was followed by learning rules, including hundreds of rules on signals alone.

She was an enthusiastic student, but every day the men tried to discourage her by making demeaning remarks, such as calling women inferior, and by telling her "horror stories" about accidents and deaths on the railroad. Linda refused to quit.

Finally, she was sent out to the freight yard to work with the equipment. "What a shock!" she remembers. She found herself jumping on and off boxcars and cranking huge handbrakes. She moved and switched cars, loading them with the right freight, which included dealing with tanker cars that were filled with chemicals or inflammable gas.

"Those cars are as big as houses," she says, "and there we were moving them around at sixty miles per hour!" She explains the dangers involved: "Imagine working on the top of a mountain. If you make a mistake up there, that could result in a potentially lethal runaway train that might instantly kill a switchman working at the bottom." From early on, Linda learned the necessity of being constantly cautious and alert.

After passing the training period, Linda worked several years in the California Salinas Valley agriculture region, called the salad bowl. She recalls being at home one afternoon in September when she received a call to report to a depot in a small yard. At the yard, she and two other crew were assigned to a produce-loading station forty miles away. They rode out in the engine of a train hauling thirty empty hopper cars, freight cars with bottoms that open for loading and unloading.

It was sugar beet season, a time when they were harvested and sent to be processed. Large truckfuls of sugar beets were steadily coming into the loading station from farms to be dumped by conveyor belt into the hopper cars. Linda and the crew threw switches and tied down brakes, delivering empty cars to a track located next to the conveyor belt. There the sugar beets were fed into the cars. Then the crew moved the cars to a siding track near the main line, to be picked up by a train that would haul the produce off to processing plants.

When a vegetable or fruit is in season, it "is running" around the clock. Crews must work fast. They work twelve-hour shifts without stopping. They work in heat, fog, and rain.

Off season, though, steady employment is hard to come by. Some railroaders become boomers, traveling to towns where there is a rush period of work.

Linda Niemann spent many years as a boomer throughout California, Oregon, Texas, Arizona, New Mexico, and Utah.

Leaving her boomer days behind, Linda Neimann works closer to home switching cars in the Southern Pacific San Jose yard.
SHIRLEY BURMAN PHOTOGRAPHER

"I've traveled on five thousand trains," she says. "Every train is different, and every day is different. The job is never boring."

But life as a boomer has its difficulties, too. Moving from town to town means being isolated and lonely. It's hard to live in a succession of strange places and make plans with family and friends. In recent years, Linda has found the life of a boomer more trying than ever. Changes in the railroad business, which has slowed down considerably, have resulted in fewer people being hired. Those still on the job are required to do more and more work that isn't part of their past specialties. Work schedules have changed drastically, as well. A brakeman is at home for ten days and then assigned to twenty days at a distant location every month.

Weary after years as a boomer, Linda Niemann has settled in Santa Cruz, California, and now works as a switchman in a yard nearby. The job is satisfying, and she continues to enjoy railroad work—outdoor work that still allows her to "do something different every day."

By the middle of the 1970s, women were breaking barriers in the workplace as they had never done before. New federal laws striking down discrimination practices against women and minorities helped immeasurably.

The story of those laws had begun a decade earlier. The United States Congress passed the Civil Rights Act of 1964, outlawing discrimination on the basis of race, color, sex, religion, and national origin in public places, voting registration practices, and in employment.

One section of the act, Title VII, created the Equal Employment Opportunity Commission (EEOC). In fact, Title VII had not been part of the original civil rights bill but was added only after women's rights activists had argued persuasively to have it included. The commission was supposed to enforce Title VII, but the agency refused to take it seriously. At the start, then, Title VII did little more than encourage employers to treat women fairly.

Years passed, and employers were *not* acting fairly. Studies showed that when discrimination complaints were filed, most charges were ignored. Women's rights groups questioned the

The brakeman knows that throwing a switch can be difficult at times for women and men. SHIRLEY BURMAN PHOTOGRAPHER

purpose of the commission and pressured the government to enforce Title VII.

Finally, in March 1972, Congress expanded the powers of the Equal Employment Opportunity Commission. The commission could force employers to comply with the law by way of court action. This stepped-up antidiscrimination drive was what had enabled Christene Gonzales to apply for engineer training on the Santa Fe.

Elsewhere, Anne Williamson, who started as a brakeman, became the first woman locomotive engineer on the Denver & Rio Grande Western. She described this railroad as "a cobweb of steel strung up and down grades, around sharp switchbacks, reverse curves, into deep canyons with fifteen-hundred-foot cliffs towering above and the Colorado River raging below." To operate a train through such territory is as challenging as railroading can get, she says, "but I love rumbling along a different world of back-yards, back roads, and back country."[3]

In California, Mary Regan rose to the position of yardmaster with the Santa Fe in Barstow when a computerized freight car classification system opened, enabling her to keep tabs on the movement of twenty-seven hundred cars a day. Julie Watson worked her way up from switchman and brakeman to freight conductor on the Southern Pacific. Barbara Perry became a bridge tender in a Southern Pacific tower high atop the Sacramento River, where she controls a double-deck railroad and a highway bridge that swivels out into the middle of the river to let vessels pass. Her job requires constant attention to train, marine, and highway traffic.[4]

Barbara McGrath didn't want to sit at a desk all day. She welcomed the opportunity to work as a switchman and brakeman on the Burlington Northern when they hired women to meet the equal employment quota. "I'm happy to be part of the new rail-road community," she says. "I'm proud that I have been able to handle the challenge of work once thought to be a man's job."[5]

Women also began stepping into management positions, as well as the growing electronic systems field. One issue of *National Business Woman* reported a new "dynamic, action-packed world for women in modern railroading." Goldie Lane rose through office ranks to become corporate secretary of the

The telegraph was replaced many years ago by newer means of communication such as radios and telephones. Today, train movements are controlled by computerized dispatching centers similar to this one in Schaumberg, Illinois. The dispatcher can check her computer screen to see where a train is and if it is on schedule.
BURLINGTON NORTHERN/SANTA FE CORPORATION

Norfolk Southern Railway, with duties ranging from handling real estate and stock market documents to business transactions. Alison Lord Boeckmann headed a team of computer specialists at Southern Pacific. Chemist Mary Pulaski worked as a spectrometric analyst for the New York Central, analyzing oil from locomotives. This helped determine which engine parts deteriorated fastest so that repairs could be anticipated and scheduled early.

Recognition of women in the "action-packed world" was welcomed, but as in the past, praise was often accompanied by patronizing comments. *National Business Woman* wrote, "There are some mighty smart women telling computers what to do!" and referred to one finance expert as "pert and alert." In 1977, a news service article on locomotive repair women began: "One of the last industrial bastions of male grit is eroding."

Although job barriers were being broken and women were gradually being allowed admission to unions, discrimination certainly didn't disappear altogether. But with the new laws, women who were unfairly treated could take legal action to win their civil rights.

In the state of Virginia, Sandra Hylton and Doris Davis took their employer, the Richmond, Fredericksburg & Potomac Railroad, to court. The women had climbed in rank and gained seniority, hoping to be accepted in an engineer training program. But every time they applied, they were turned down. The railroad made one excuse after another.

Ten years passed. During that period, the railroad hired forty-two men as engineer trainees, some with less seniority than the women. Finally, Sandra and Doris filed a sex discrimination suit against the railroad.

When the case came to court in 1984, the railroad argued that

the women weren't physically strong enough to operate locomotives. The women, represented by their lawyer, maintained
that while stamina and concentration were necessary for all engineers, extraordinary physical capabilities were not. The judge
ruled that the railroad was guilty.

Sandra Hylton and Doris Davis won their case in court but not
their rightful chance at engineer training. The railroad still didn't
want to take them on and offered them so much money to retire
that they eventually settled the case and left.

Another case, one filed in California, had had a different out-
come. Leah Rosenfeld had gone to work as a telegrapher for the
Southern Pacific during World War II. She continued after
the war, and her work changed with the new technology, giving
her the titles of train order operator and wire chief. Throughout
that time, she was the sole supporter of her family.

After eleven years, in 1955, she applied for promotion as agent
of a station, which included being in charge of other station
employees. She was rejected then and at every attempt that fol
lowed. Leah filed a sex-discrimination suit against the railroad
and the state of California, citing a state labor law that "pro-
tected" women by disallowing them to work more than eight
hours a day or lift more than twenty-five pounds. Through her
lawyer, Leah argued that she had gained seniority and that she
needed a salary raise to support her family. She testified that
she already worked beyond eight-hour days and lifted weights
greater than twenty-five pounds. She would have risked being
fired if she didn't do her job as required.

The case was delayed for years while it was appealed to higher
courts. At last, a U.S. circuit court heard the case and ruled in
Leah Rosenfeld's favor. Not only did she win a legal victory but

she also won a job as agent at a station, a promotion she had long deserved.

CHANGING TIMES IN TRANSPORTATION

While changes were occurring for women railroaders, the entire industry itself was undergoing a drastic transformation. This had begun in the late 1940s, after World War II, when the nation experienced a shift from wartime to peacetime economy, and the railroad was no longer so urgently needed.

The United States, in its prosperous postwar days, built a vast interstate highway system. Automobile sales rose dramatically. Long-distance trucking was used increasingly to haul freight. Aircraft design improved, and with government support, passenger air travel took off.

Railroads suffered serious losses. They tried to survive by merging companies and pooling revenues, but that wasn't enough. Finally, the industry sought help from the government. In 1971, the U.S. Congress created the National Railroad Passenger Corporation to run all intercity trains, using tracks owned by the freight railroads. The passenger service of Amtrak was born.

At first, Amtrak hired women mostly in clerical and personal service jobs, but slowly, the women began to advance to other levels. And in time, the majority joined one of several trade union organizations, such as the Brotherhood of Locomotive Engineers, Railroad Yardmasters of America, and the American Federation of Railroad Police, Inc.

One woman, Lillian Tamoria,[6] went to work as an Amtrak sales agent in California and soon developed a "passion and loyalty to the railroad." Later, she was promoted to Manager, Customer Services in the western division Los Angeles office, where she remains today. She oversees policy, budget, and personnel in special service departments that handle express shipments, group ticket sales, and the needs of physically disabled travelers, such as arranging for wheelchairs, ramps, and extra space on board for wheelchair-bound passengers. She also plans excursion train rides for school and scout groups.

NEW POWER, GROWING STRENGTH

Across the nation today, some 27,000 women work for railroads. about 8 percent of all railroaders.

The last time they were counted by job category was in 1983. In that year, 38,825 women were employed. Listed under *female* were:

777 engineers, conductors, brakemen, and switchmen
1,928 maintenance workers
31,722 general clerical, executive office, and supervisory personnel

Currently, there are some 530 railroad companies, nine of which are major railroads. The rest are regional or local.

Women now fill positions in such divisions as financial planning, insurance, and employee benefits. They manage computer programs and analyses, information technology, communications, and train operations. They direct departments in marketing and public relations. They are executive vice presidents, railroad attorneys, civil engineers, environmental specialists, and safety coordinators.

One executive remarked that women are advancing more readily in management than in train operations because women in general are widely succeeding in areas of economics,

SHE'S BEEN WORKING ON THE RAILROAD

At dusk in the desert town of Carlin, Nevada, engineer Susan Gibson is switching freight cars in the rail yard before taking her train eastbound to Ogden, Utah. SHIRLEY BURMAN PHOTOGRAPHER

The 20-below-zero weather did not prevent these new railroad recruits from posing for a public relations photo. SANTA FE RAILWAY

As a carman, Doris Ford works in a rail yard inspecting freight car wheels for worn brake shoes that need to be replaced. SHIRLEY BURMAN PHOTOGRAPHER

computers, and marketing. "Train operations often *does* mean hard and dirty work," she says, but she adds, "all of us must come to accept the right of women to opt for work in operations divisions, too, if that is what they choose."[7]

Meanwhile, women continue to achieve success in the corporate railroad world. Anne Hazell,[8] civil engineer, works in Washington, D.C., at the Association of American Railroads (AAR), an organization that represents major U.S. railroads as well as railroads in Canada and Mexico. In her past position as Director of Engineering, she consulted in track and bridge design and construction, inspected flood damage, and consulted with federal agencies when problems arose. In 1995, she was promoted to Assistant to the Executive Vice President. Working in financial management now, she is responsible for an annual budget of twelve million dollars.

Magda Ratajski, of the Norfolk Southern Railway in Norfolk, Virginia, was one of the industry's first women to be named a corporate vice president. Now, as Vice President, Public Relations, she is responsible for communications, advertising, marketing, and budgeting in those departments. A primary concern is to bring in customers—companies that select and use railroads to ship their freight, ranging from coal, grain, and plastics to automobiles and auto parts.

Magda likes the "different dimensions" of her work. One day she may be at the computer or developing an advertising campaign. Another, she may be flying across the country to attend a meeting. Or she may be purchasing a railroad painting, photograph, or collectible artifact like a valuable old lantern or track spike to add to the Norfolk Southern's treasured Americana railroad collection.

SHE'S BEEN WORKING ON THE RAILROAD

Maggie Silver's[9] father bought his first of several railroads in 1938. It was the Hoosac Tunnel & Wilmington, sometimes called the Hoot, Toot, & Whistle. It hauled freight on several short lines that connected with long-distance carriers. Maggie's father was happy to have his daughter work there. But only in the office. As much as Maggie wanted to experience train operations, her father said, "No, that is not appropriate for a girl."

When he died, Maggie was advised to sell the company. She had come to appreciate and love the business, though, and she did not sell. Instead, in 1977, she took over as president.

The company, called the Pinsly, now owns six short-line railroads and three reload stations, terminals that have freight distribution centers. The short lines run in Massachusetts, Arkansas, South Carolina, and Florida. They haul freight with Pinsly's twenty diesel locomotives, which are painted red with yellow lettering identifying each of the lines.

As president, Maggie Silver heads financial and legal departments. She meets with government representatives who set railroad and freight regulations. She travels to inspect her six railroads. Her top priority is customer service, making sure that present freight customers are satisfied. She also continually seeks new ones. In recent years, she has met with much success in strengthening and expanding her business.

After more than two decades leading a multimillion-dollar company, Maggie says that from time to time she still experiences bias against women. On occasion when she walks into a conference room, she finds herself ignored by some of the men, at least until they learn who she is. For the most part, though, she believes that she is welcomed in the industry because she has worked hard and earned her place.

Maggie has four grown children; one son works for the company. She also has five grandchildren, three boys and two girls, giving her hope that yet another generation might carry on the legacy of the family railroad, if that should be their choice. "I especially want to give the girls a chance to learn all aspects of the business early in their lives, a privilege I didn't have when I was young," Maggie Silver says. "I would like to see *all* my grandchildren experience the good living, reward, and fulfillment that the railroad has given me."

It has been a century and a half since the story of railroad women began.

Some of those women came to railroading by way of family. Some were driven by economic need, while others answered a call to patriotic duty. And some felt a strong desire for active, outdoor work.

No matter how or when they opted for a railroad job or career, in the end that was the industry they chose. Once there, all of them met unique challenges.

Barriers continue to be broken, but prejudice, stereotyping, and resistance still exist. Now women ask: Will the time come when they are accepted equally in management and in train operations? Will their opportunities equal those afforded to men without having to wage legal battles to win them? Will a woman become president of a major railroad?

More and more people favor such progressive change, although there are still many who are strongly opposed. But women, as well as men, who want to experience new horizons, who dream of traveling new roads, ought to have the right to make that choice.

Endnotes

Chapter 1   BRASS POUNDERS

1. Stewart H. Holbrook, *The Story of American Railroads* (New York: Crown, 1947), p. 64.
2. *The Eagle*, Vinton, Iowa, December 2, 1874.
3. *The Autobiography of Andrew Carnegie* (New York: Houghton Mifflin, 1920), pp. 66–67.
4. *The Telegrapher*, July 1876.

Chapter 2   INTO THE TWENTIETH CENTURY

1. Marvin E. Locke, "The Trail, Nevada County Narrow Gauge, an Historical Thesis," 1963.
2. Barbara Heggie, "Ice Woman," *The New Yorker* (September 6, 1941), pp. 23–29.
3. Ida Stevens Petersen, interview, Costa Mesa, California, May 1996.
4. Lesley Poling-Kempes, *The Harvey Girls: Women Who Opened the West* (New York: Paragon House, 1989), pp. 65–67.
5. Elbert Hubbard, "The Fra." Quote noted by Pamela Berkman in "The Fred Harvey Story," *All Aboard! The Golden Age of American Railroad Travel*, Bill Yenne, editor (New York: Barnes and Noble, 1989), p. 40.
6. Drawings contained at Little Bighorn Battlefield National Monument Museum, Crow Agency, Montana.
7. Virginia L. Grattan, *Mary Colter: Builder Upon the Red Earth* (Grand Canyon, Arizona: Grand Canyon Natural History Association, 1992), p. 2.
8. Ibid., p. 19.

Chapter 3   WORLD WAR I

1. *B & O Magazine*, August 1957, p. 42.
2. Maurine Weiner Greenwald, *Women, War, and Work: The Impact of*

ENDNOTES

World War I on Women Workers in the United States (Westport, Connecticut: Greenwood Press, 1980), p. 97.

3. *The B & O Bulletin*, April 1919, p. 16.
4. Greenwald, p. 131.

Chapter 4   NURSES AND HOSTESSES ON BOARD

1. Ruth Morgan Weitkamp, interview, Seattle, Washington, March 1996.
2. *Southern Pacific Bulletin*, May 1941, p. 9.
3. "UP's Nurse-Stewardesses: Nightingales of the Rails," *Infomagazine*, July/August 1991, p. 22.

Chapter 5   WORLD WAR II

1. Mary Ellen Cookman Day, interview, Los Angeles, California, June 1996.
2. Stuart Leuthner, *Railroaders* (New York: Random House, 1983), pp. 38–43.
3. Laura Nelson Baker, *Wanted: Women in War Industry* (New York: Dutton, 1943), p. 72.
4. Jocelyn Wagner Knowles, interview, Sarasota, Florida, April 1996.

Chapter 6   YESTERDAY, TODAY, AND TOMORROW

1. Christene Gonzales Alders, interview, El Paso, Texas, April 1996.
2. Linda Niemann, interview, Santa Cruz, California, March 1996; *Boomer* (Berkeley: University of California Press), 1990.
3. Anne Williamson, "Driving the Rails: A Woman's Journey," *Denver Magazine*, March 1982, pp. 42–45.
4. Julie Watson and Barbara Perry, interviews, Sacramento, California, March 1996.
5. Barbara McGrath, "Brakeperson Makes Career out of 'Man's' Job," *Missoulian*, July 12, 1992, p. 9.
6. Lillian Tamoria, interview, Los Angeles, California, June 1996.
7. Magda Ratajski, interview, Norfolk, Virginia, July 1996.
8. Anne Hazell, interview, Washington, D.C., June 1996.
9. Maggie Silver, interview, Westfield, Massachusetts, July 1996. Further material from Liane Enkelis and Karen Olsen, *On Our Own Terms* (San Francisco: Berrett-Koehler, 1995), pp. 135–143.

Glossary

Boomer worker who is hired in places where needed

Brakeman person who couples and uncouples cars and works the brakes when a car is free rolling

Brass pounder telegraph operator; also called an op

Car rail vehicle in which passengers travel or in which freight is carried; box-car is roofed and square-walled, with sliding doors

Conductor train boss; keeps track of schedules, collects tickets, and is in charge of passenger needs and employee conduct

Cornfield meet head-on collision

Couple means for connecting cars to an engine or cars to each other

Dispatcher worker who sends off trains on schedule

Doubleheader train hauled by two engines

Engineer person who operates a locomotive; also hogger or hoghead

Fireman worker who shovels coal and pitches cordwood into firebox to be sure locomotive has enough steam

Flagman trainman who protects the standing train's rear

Gandy dancer pick-and-shovel track repairman

Hopper steel-sided freight car that opens on the bottom to allow loading and unloading

Locomotive engine (also called a hog) that makes its own power to move; locomotives of past years were powered by steam; today they operate mostly by diesel and electric power

Morse code signal system using dots and dashes, or short and long sounds, to represent letters of the alphabet; sent and received by operators over telegraph wires and "translated" into messages

Narrow-gauge railway trains and tracks of less than the standard gauge size of 4 feet and 8.5 inches between the two track rails

Reefer refrigerator car

Rolling stock all locomotives, rail cars, and other railroad vehicles

Roundhouse place where engines are inspected and repaired

96

GLOSSARY

Signals means of controlling train movement; signals are given by arm and hand, lantern, electric-light semaphore, engine whistle, and radio

Switchman person in charge of railroad switches at a junction or siding; also helps in moving and making up trains

Throttle valve that regulates the flow of steam, gasoline, or other fuel to operate an engine; full or open throttle is to go full speed

Trestle supportive framework of wood, iron, or steel, used as a railroad bridge for trains crossing over a gap

Trick eight-hour work shift

Yard system of tracks for making up trains or storing cars

Further Reading

Best, Gerald M. *Nevada County Narrow Gauge*. Berkeley: Howell-North Books, 1965.

Browne, Juanita Kennedy. *A Tale of Two Cities and a Train*. Nevada City: Nevada County History Society, 1987.

Bryant, Keith Jr. *History of the Atchison, Topeka and Santa Fe*. New York: Macmillan, 1974.

Foner, Philip S. *Women and the American Labor Movement*. New York: Free Press, Macmillan, 1980.

Gabler, Edwin. *The American Telegrapher: A Social History, 1860–1900*. New Brunswick, New Jersey: Rutgers University Press, 1988.

Grattan, Virginia L. *Mary Colter: Builder Upon the Red Earth*. Grand Canyon, Arizona: Grand Canyon Natural History Association, 1992.

Greenwald, Maurine Weiner. *Women, War, and Work: The Impact of World War I on Women Workers in the United States*. Westport, Connecticut: Greenwood Press, 1980.

———. "Women Workers and World War I: The American Railroad Industry, A Case Study," *Journal of Social History*, Vol. 9, Winter, 1975.

Holbrook, Stewart H. *The Story of American Railroads*. New York: Crown, 1947.

Knowles, Jocelyn. "The Lady Brakeman," *American Heritage*, July/August 1995.

Lathrop, Carl. "Where the Girls Were," *National Railway Bulletin*, Vol. 58, No. 6, 1993.

Licht, Walter. *Working on the Railroad: The Organization of Work in the 19th Century*. Princeton, New Jersey: Princeton University Press, 1983.

FURTHER READING

Morris, Juddi. *The Harvey Girls: The Women Who Civilized the West*. New York: Walker and Co., 1994.

Poling-Kempes, Lesley. *The Harvey Girls: Women Who Opened the West*. New York: Paragon House, 1989.

Sanders, D. G. *The Brass Pounder*. New York: Hawthorn Books, 1978.

White, John H. *The Great Yellow Fleet: A History of American Refrigerator Cars*. San Marino, California: Golden West Books, 1986.

Withuhn, William, ed. *Rails Across America: A History of Railroads in North America*. Washington, D.C.: Smithsonian Institution, 1993.

Index

Page numbers in *italics* refer to photos.

INDEX

INDEX

INDEX

INDEX